REVIEW OF THREE DIVISIONS OF THE INFORMATION TECHNOLOGY LABORATORY AT THE NATIONAL INSTITUTE OF STANDARDS AND TECHNOLOGY

FISCAL YEAR 2015

Panel on Review of the Information Technology Laboratory at the National Institute of Standards and Technology

Committee on NIST Technical Programs

Laboratory Assessments Board

Division on Engineering and Physical Sciences

The National Academies of
SCIENCES · ENGINEERING · MEDICINE

THE NATIONAL ACADEMIES PRESS
Washington, D.C.
www.nap.edu

THE NATIONAL ACADEMIES PRESS   500 Fifth Street, NW   Washington, DC 20001

This study was supported by Contract No. SB1341-12-CQ-0036/15-034 between the National Academy of Sciences and the National Institute of Standards and Technology. Any opinions, findings, conclusions, or recommendations expressed in this publication do not necessarily reflect the views of any organization or agency that provided support for the project.

International Standard Book Number-13: 978-0-309-38906-8
International Standard Book Number-10: 0-309-38906-2

Copies of this report are available from

Laboratory Assessments Board
Division on Engineering and Physical Sciences
National Academies of Sciences, Engineering, and Medicine
500 Fifth Street, NW
Keck 928
Washington, DC 20001

Additional copies of this report are available from the National Academies Press, 500 Fifth Street, NW, Keck 360, Washington, DC 20001; (800) 624-6242 or (202) 334-3313; http://www.nap.edu.

Copyright 2015 by the National Academies of Sciences, Engineering, and Medicine. All rights reserved.

Printed in the United States of America

Suggested Citation: National Academies of Sciences, Engineering, and Medicine. 2015. *Review of Three Divisions of the Information Technology Laboratory at the National Institute of Standards and Technology: Fiscal Year 2015.* Washington, DC: The National Academies Press.

The National Academies of
SCIENCES · ENGINEERING · MEDICINE

The **National Academy of Sciences** was established in 1863 by an Act of Congress, signed by President Lincoln, as a private, nongovernmental institution to advise the nation on issues related to science and technology. Members are elected by their peers for outstanding contributions to research. Dr. Ralph J. Cicerone is president.

The **National Academy of Engineering** was established in 1964 under the charter of the National Academy of Sciences to bring the practices of engineering to advising the nation. Members are elected by their peers for extraordinary contributions to engineering. Dr. C. D. Mote, Jr., is president.

The **National Academy of Medicine** (formerly the Institute of Medicine) was established in 1970 under the charter of the National Academy of Sciences to advise the nation on medical and health issues. Members are elected by their peers for distinguished contributions to medicine and health. Dr. Victor J. Dzau is president.

The three Academies work together as the **National Academies of Sciences, Engineering, and Medicine** to provide independent, objective analysis and advice to the nation and conduct other activities to solve complex problems and inform public policy decisions. The Academies also encourage education and research, recognize outstanding contributions to knowledge, and increase public understanding in matters of science, engineering, and medicine.

Learn more about the National Academies of Sciences, Engineering, and Medicine at **www.national-academies.org.**

PANEL ON REVIEW OF THE INFORMATION TECHNOLOGY LABORATORY AT THE NATIONAL INSTITUTE OF STANDARDS AND TECHNOLOGY

CONSTANTINE GATSONIS, Brown University, *Chair*
DON EUGENE DETMER, University of Virginia
PETER T. HIGGINS, Higgins & Associates, International
GERARD J. HOLZMANN, NASA Jet Propulsion Laboratory
NIKIL S. JAYANT, University of California, Santa Barbara
KAREN KAFADAR, University of Virginia
JAMES M. LANDWEHR, Avaya Laboratories
GARY MARCHIONINI, University of North Carolina, Chapel Hill
MITCHELL P. MARCUS, University of Pennsylvania
MICHAEL MULLER, IBM Research
PHILIP M. NECHES, Teradata Corporation
J. MARC OVERHAGE, Cerner Corporation
GEORGE J. PAPPAS, University of Pennsylvania
DANIEL A. REED, University of Iowa
JOEL SALTZ, Stony Brook University
ALBERTO SANGIOVANNI-VINCENTELLI, University of California, Berkeley
WILLIAM L. SCHERLIS, Carnegie Mellon University
STEPHANIE A.C. SCHUCKERS, Clarkson University
PETER TU, General Electric Global Research
STEPHEN B. VARDEMAN, Iowa State University

Staff

LIZA HAMILTON, Associate Program Officer
EVA LABRE, Administrative Coordinator
JAMES P. McGEE, Director
ANDREA SHELTON, Administrative Assistant

COMMITTEE ON NIST TECHNICAL PROGRAMS

ELSA REICHMANIS, Georgia Institute of Technology, *Chair*
LEWIS BRANSCOMB, Harvard University
WILLIAM C. GEAR, NEC Research Institute, Inc. (retired)
JENNIE S. HWANG, H-Technologies Group
KANTI JAIN, University of Illinois, Urbana-Champaign
C. KUMAR N. PATEL, Pranalytica, Inc.
ALICE WHITE, Boston University

Staff

LIZA HAMILTON, Associate Program Officer
EVA LABRE, Administrative Coordinator
JAMES P. McGEE Director
ANDREA SHELTON, Administrative Assistant

LABORATORY ASSESSMENTS BOARD

JOHN W. LYONS, National Defense University, *Chair*
ROSS B. COROTIS, University of Colorado, Boulder
PAUL A. FLEURY, Yale University
C. WILLIAM GEAR, Princeton University
WESLEY L. HARRIS, Massachusetts Institute of Technology
JENNIE S. HWANG, H-Technologies Group
W. CARL LINE BERGER, University of Colorado, Boulder
C. KUMAR N. PATEL, Pranalytica, Inc.
ELSA REICHMANIS, Georgia Institute of Technology
LYLE H. SCHWARTZ, U.S. Air Force Office of Scientific Research (retired)

Staff

LIZA HAMILTON, Associate Program Officer
EVA LABRE, Administrative Coordinator
JAMES P. McGEE, Director
ARUL MOZHI, Senior Program Officer
ANDREA SHELTON, Administrative Assistant

Acknowledgment of Reviewers

This report has been reviewed in draft form by individuals chosen for their diverse perspectives and technical expertise, in accordance with procedures approved by the Report Review Committee. The purpose of this independent review is to provide candid and critical comments that will assist the institution in making its published report as sound as possible and to ensure that the report meets institutional standards for objectivity, evidence, and responsiveness to the study charge. The review comments and draft manuscript remain confidential to protect the integrity of the deliberative process. We wish to thank the following individuals for their review of this report:

Philip A. Bernstein, Microsoft Corporation,
Luis A. Escobar, Louisiana State University,
C. William Gear, NEC Research Institute, Inc.,
Michael Lesk, Rutgers, The State University of New Jersey,
Alexa T. McCray, Harvard Medical School,
Richard Pew, Raytheon BBN Technologies, and
David Scott, Rice University.

Although the reviewers listed above have provided many constructive comments and suggestions, they were not asked to endorse the conclusions or recommendations, nor did they see the final draft of the report before its release. The review of this report was overseen by David E. Crow, University of Connecticut, who was responsible for making certain that an independent examination of this report was carried out in accordance with institutional procedures and that all review comments were carefully considered. Responsibility for the final content of this report rests entirely with the authoring panel and the institution.

Contents

SUMMARY		1
1	THE CHARGE TO THE PANEL AND THE ASSESSMENT PROCESS	7
2	INFORMATION ACCESS DIVISION	9
3	STATISTICAL ENGINEERING DIVISION	16
4	SOFTWARE AND SYSTEMS DIVISION	20
ACRONYMS		29

Summary

At the request of the Director of the National Institute of Standards and Technology (NIST), in 2015 the National Research Council[1] formed the Panel on Review of the Information Technology Laboratory at the National Institute of Standards and Technology and formulated the following statement of task for the panel:

> The National Research Council shall appoint a panel to assess the scientific and technical work performed by the National Institute of Standards and Technology (NIST) Information Technology Laboratory. This panel will review technical reports and technical program descriptions prepared by NIST staff and will visit the facilities at the Information Technology Laboratory. Visits will include technical presentations by NIST staff, demonstrations of NIST projects, tours of NIST facilities, and discussions with NIST staff. The panel will prepare a report summarizing its assessment findings.

NIST specified that three of the six divisions of the Information Technology Laboratory (ITL) would be reviewed: the Information Access Division (IAD), the Software and Systems Division (SSD), and the Statistical Engineering Division (SED). The following ITL divisions were not reviewed because they had recently been reorganized: the Applied and Computational Mathematics Division, the Computer Security Division, and the Advanced Networking Technologies Division. NIST plans to request their review in the future. The NIST Director requested that the panel focus its assessment on the following factors:

1. Assess the organization's technical programs.
   - How does the quality of the research compare to similar world class research in the technical program areas?
   - Is the quality of the technical programs adequate for the organization to reach its stated technical objectives? How could it be improved?
2. Assess the portfolio of scientific expertise within the organization.
   - Does the organization have world-class scientific expertise in the areas of the organization's mission and program objectives? If not, what areas should be improved?
   - How well does the organization's scientific expertise support the organization's technical programs and the organization's ability to achieve its stated objectives?
3. Assess the adequacy of the organization's facilities, equipment, and human resources.
   - How well do the facilities, equipment, and human resources support the organization's technical programs and its ability to achieve its stated objectives? How could they be improved?
4. Assess the effectiveness by which the organization disseminates its program outputs.
   - How well are the organization's research programs driven by stakeholder needs?
   - How effective are the technology transfer mechanisms used by the organization? Are

---

[1] Effective July 1, 2015, the institution is called the National Academies of Sciences, Engineering, and Medicine. References in this report to the National Research Council are used in an historical context identifying programs prior to July 1.

- these mechanisms sufficiently comprehensive?
- How well is the organization monitoring stakeholder use and impact of program outputs? How could this be improved?

This summary presents general observations about the ITL divisions reviewed and observations and recommendations specific to the divisions reviewed.

GENERAL OBSERVATIONS

ITL has a unique role as convener and facilitator of research and technology development. This role of the Laboratory and, more broadly, of NIST, is of great importance to the nation. ITL has a very broad range of projects, some with significant influence on public policy, such as the projects on voting, health-related information technology, forensics, and cyberphysical and cybersecurity systems. Resources are spread thin, even in these key projects. As described below, each division faces special challenges with respect to needed expertise and numbers of researchers. While there was modest evidence of a systematic, data-driven process of planning for personnel and resources, both short- and long-term, this planning needs improvement.

The ability to respond successfully to mandates and to generate new research projects in support of its core mission is essential to ITL. There was modest evidence of systematic horizon-scanning in the realms of government, industry, and the sciences, but ITL needs to improve its horizon scanning.

The role of convener and facilitator of research and technology development is a major part of ITL's contribution. However, ITL's outreach activities do not seem to make optimal use of current Internet-based capabilities.

DIVISION-SPECIFIC OBSERVATIONS, CONCLUSIONS, AND RECOMMENDATIONS

Information Access Division

The technical programs in the IAD are, in general, well organized, well staffed, and appropriate to the mission of ITL and to the IAD itself. The research teams enjoy broad peer recognition while supporting the NIST mission. The core competencies and facilities in this division are strong, and interactions with other parts of ITL and NIST are evident, if not always formalized. It is important that while maintaining momentum and leadership the IAD also consider enhancing engagement in new opportunities in areas such as data-driven information science, security policy, and health informatics. There was modest evidence of ongoing critical review of programs.

The portfolio of scientific expertise is appropriate and impressive for the traditional areas that the IAD focuses on, but core capabilities need to be enhanced in areas where the IAD aspires to make a major contribution.

Recommendation 1: The Information Access Division should review the current and proposed portfolios and examine the adequacy of its core competencies for ambitious new programs like data science, health informatics, and public safety.

Supporting the standards process places resource and attention-span demands on personnel. One option to reduce the demands could be to turn over standards materials to the International Organization for Standardization (ISO) and other standards development organizations (SDOs). However, this approach is sometimes associated with update cycles that are too long and possibly too onerous to meet the original intent of the standard, and it entails risk to IAD credibility.

Recommendation 2: The Information Access Division (IAD) should continually consider the pros and cons of turning over standards materials—for example, the Common Industry Format (CIF)—to the International Organization for Standardization (ISO) and other standards development organizations (SDOs). If the ISO-SDO channel remains the best or only approach, the IAD should consider how to plan proactively for updates as appropriate and should propose updates to the controlling SDO(s) whenever IAD efforts indicate they are needed or desired by the user community.

Facilities, equipment, and human resources are strong assets of IAD. As areas such as health informatics gain importance, there seems to be a tendency to make do with the existing core talent areas rather than hiring specialists—for example, trained biomedical informaticians and health data scientists—permanently or even for shorter periods of time. This practice needs to be reconsidered during strategic planning for the division. A prime example of where such expertise is needed is the electronic health record team.

Recommendation 3: The Information Access Division (IAD) should bolster the electronic health record team to ensure that this high-profile work is well supported in terms of information technology rigor as well as domain expertise. IAD should add scientists or contractors with strong clinical experience, include all stakeholders (physicians, nurses, technicians, pharmacists, and patients) in its empirical investigations, and participate in medical informatics communities such the American Medical Informatics Association(AMIA) and the congressionally chartered Patient-Centered Outcomes Research Institute (PCORI). Internally, the IAD should collaborate closely with the Text Retrieval Conference (TREC) team on medical tracks.

Collaborative teamwork with scientists and engineers inside and outside IAD, including virtual teamwork and in-person interactions, is of fundamental importance to the work of the IAD staff.

Recommendation 4: To maximize the mechanism of virtual teams and to foster contacts with other laboratories, the Information Access Division should give greater consideration to the formulation of clear policies and processes that support sabbaticals and appropriate travel.

The IAD value proposition with standards and conformance toolsets is outstanding and deserves continued nurturing and support. Its dissemination process would be enhanced by greater use of Internet-based methods.

Recommendation 5: The Information Access Division should apply more Internet-based methods to its dissemination and outreach process. Such methods as webinars, virtual meetings, and recordings should be considered.

Statistical Engineering Division

The SED is well-aligned and effective in its support of ITL and NIST missions. The division's portfolio includes a wide variety of projects, including classical statistical metrology projects such as those on mass calibration weighing designs. Other work supports national and international best statistical practices in metrology and the development of new methods of measurement and uncertainty quantification for important specialized technical applications. The SED efforts are technically challenging and well executed. The division's scientific expertise in statistics for metrology continues to be among the best in the world. The SED continues to have a low profile in the national and international technical statistics community. If this profile were to be enhanced, SED could more fully benefit from and contribute to current statistical research.

> **Recommendation 6: The Statistical Engineering Division should take steps to raise its profile through technical publications in statistics venues and through educational efforts to improve the awareness of statistics educators of the vital role of measurement in data collection and the role of statistics in good measurement.**

Attention to both metrology and the basic statistics field needs to be a division priority to move both areas forward and guarantee ongoing excellence in supporting NIST priorities.

> **Recommendation 7: The Statistical Engineering Division should seek stronger ties with the statistical research community in terms of both publications and human resources.**

Progress has been made on human resource issues, but important challenges remain to provide technical staffing on important projects and in critical areas, as well as to anticipate future staff losses with potential retirement.

> **Recommendation 8: In hiring permanent employees, the Statistical Engineering Division (SED) should focus attention on (1) ensuring corporate memory of and expertise in the fundamental ongoing National Institute of Standards and Technology (NIST) standard reference material (SRM), calibration, and the experimental design work that has always been part of the SED portfolio, and on developing new capabilities in priority areas such as shape metrology and greenhouse gas monitoring, which seem to be particularly thinly staffed; (2) maintaining high overall technical competence; (3) improving staff diversity; and (4) balancing emphases on the noncore and core areas—for example, while forensics is a current laboratory-wide priority and SED is a key participant, when hiring for forensics the SED should address general expertise, so that other more thinly staffed critical areas are not neglected.**

> **Recommendation 9: The Statistical Engineering Division should invigorate its program of graduate student internships to include two to four Ph.D. students per summer, and it should begin to develop a much broader and stronger program of visiting faculty researchers.**

Publications, presentations, interacting with visiting researchers, and sponsoring interns are important means for engaging with the statistical and metrology communities.

> **Recommendation 10: The Statistical Engineering Division should monitor its yearly division total publications in the three categories—subject-matter journals, metrology journals, and statistics journals—and external research presentations, research visitor days, and internships sponsored.**

Software and Systems Division

The SSD is engaged in several high profile areas, notably in voting, health information technology (IT), and cyberphysical systems (CPS). It is crucial that the SSD, in collaboration with ITL and NIST management, delineate the risks and rewards of each area in the context of organizational strategy. By defining the stakeholders and success metrics, it can match competence and resources to the risks and rewards.

The SSD work on cloud computing standards has had substantial government and industry impact, both within the United States and internationally. The NIST cloud-computing reference architecture is now internationally accepted, and it has led to a voluntary, consensus ISO standard.

The SSD group working on computational metrology has been successful in attracting strong scientific collaborators in the stem-cell therapy area and in collaborations that have generated both publicly distributed software and published scientific results. The group's focus could be expanded to a broader set of areas. The inherent strengths of the SSD in computational metrology might be better served by a sharper focus on metrology methodology issues and metrology-related imaging standards.

The SSD group working on voting security and verification has played a major role in voting systems development and implementation for more than a decade. The group has a low public profile that is not commensurate with its contribution.

The SSD work on software assurance has produced useful data sets that can benefit the producers of software tools. The group has also had success in raising awareness about the existence of these data sets, including databases of common software risks and security vulnerabilities, and the existence of test cases. The group's portfolio of activities could benefit from closer alignment with the work of other ITL units. More could be done by the SSD to develop effective software test tools and methodologies and to disseminate them—for example, for conformance and interoperability testing. The SSD could take a leading role in the development of software test tools.

The SSD group working on cyberphysical systems and the Internet of Things has developed a technically sound portfolio of activity that addresses some of the important issues in the area. The group has demonstrated leadership by launching projects such as the smart city grand challenge and the Cyber-Physical Systems Public Working Group (CPS PWG). The recognition and engagement with the scientific community gained by the SSD in this area is not yet matched by a similar level of visibility and engagement in the industrial community.

The SSD group addressing electronic health records is working hard to respond to challenging mandates from the Office of the National Coordinator (ONC). However, it is not clear how the needs of the continuously evolving ONC strategy can best be addressed by ITL in a sustainable way. The current staff comprises capable computer scientists and information technologists but includes no biomedical/health informaticians.

It would be beneficial for the SSD to increase its engagement with the scientific and industrial communities.

Recommendation 11: The Software and Systems Division not only should participate with the International Organization for Standardization (ISO)/International Electrotechnical Commission (IEC) joint technical committee working group on the Internet of Things (ISO/IEC JTC 1/WG 10) and the Institute of Electrical and Electronics Engineers (IEEE) project on the Standard for an Architectural Framework for the Internet of Things (P2413), but also should reach out to industrial consortia such as the Industrial Internet Consortium and the Open Interconnect Consortium.

Recommendation 12: The Software and Systems Division should make open to the scientific and industrial communities the framework that it put together for the Smart Grid, as well as tools and techniques developed in university projects such as Precision Timed (PRET) machines project at the University of California, Berkeley.

Recommendation 13: The Software and Systems Division should look into growing its approach to timing in connection with Internet of Things applications by considering protocols that are robust to clock drift.

It is not clear that the ONC has a comprehensive strategy that allocates the tasks needed for the nation to achieve interoperable EHRs and EHR systems. Within this context, the SSD is faced with making strategic choices as to the most effective focus for its EHR work.

Recommendation 14: For electronic health records (EHRs) the Software and Systems Division (SSD) should define a clear direction that allows it to either focus on limited objectives or add staff of the appropriate types to meet larger expectations. Because focusing on meaningful use of EHRs is intrinsically clinical in nature, the SSD should consider adding clinical informaticians to its staff.

1

The Charge to the Panel and the Assessment Process

At the request of the National Institute of Standards and Technology (NIST), the National Research Council (NRC)[1] has, since 1959, annually assembled panels of experts from academia, industry, medicine, and other scientific and engineering environments to assess the quality and effectiveness of the NIST measurements and standards laboratories, of which there are now seven,[2] as well as the adequacy of the laboratories' resources.

At the request of the Director of NIST, in 2015 the NRC formed the Panel on Review of the Information Technology Laboratory at the National Institute of Standards and Technology and established the following statement of task for the panel:

> The National Research Council [National Academies of Sciences, Engineering, and Medicine] shall appoint a panel to assess the scientific and technical work performed by the National Institute of Standards and Technology (NIST) Information Technology Laboratory. This panel will review technical reports and technical program descriptions prepared by NIST staff and will visit the facilities at the Information Technology Laboratory. Visits will include technical presentations by NIST staff, demonstrations of NIST projects, tours of NIST facilities, and discussions with NIST staff. The panel will prepare a report summarizing its assessment findings.

The NIST Director requested that the panel focus its assessment on the following factors:

1. Assess the organization's technical programs.
   - How does the quality of the research compare to similar world class research in the technical program areas?
   - Is the quality of the technical programs adequate for the organization to reach its stated technical objectives? How could it be improved?
2. Assess the portfolio of scientific expertise within the organization.
   - Does the organization have world-class scientific expertise in the areas of the organization's mission and program objectives? If not, what areas should be improved?
   - How well does the organization's scientific expertise support the organization's technical programs and the organization's ability to achieve its stated objectives?
3. Assess the adequacy of the organization's facilities, equipment, and human resources
   - How well do the facilities, equipment, and human resources support the organization's technical programs and its ability to achieve its stated objectives? How could they be improved?

---

[1] Effective July 1, 2015, the institution is called the National Academies of Sciences, Engineering, and Medicine. References in this report to the National Research Council are used in an historical context identifying programs prior to July 1.

[2] The seven NIST laboratories are the Engineering Laboratory, the Physical Measurement Laboratory, the Information Technology Laboratory, the Material Measurement Laboratory, the Communication Technology Laboratory, the Center for Nanoscale Science and Technology, and the NIST Center for Neutron Research.

4. Assess the effectiveness by which the organization disseminates its program outputs.
   - How well are the organization's research programs driven by stakeholder needs?
   - How effective are the technology transfer mechanisms used by the organization? Are these mechanisms sufficiently comprehensive?
   - How well is the organization monitoring stakeholder use and impact of program outputs? How could this be improved?

The context of this technical assessment is the mission of NIST, which is to promote U.S. innovation and industrial competitiveness by advancing measurement science, standards, and technology in ways that enhance economic security and improve the quality of life. The NIST laboratories conduct research to anticipate future metrology and standards needs, enable new scientific and technological advances, and improve and refine existing measurement methods and services.

NIST specified that three of the six divisions of the Information Technology Laboratory (ITL) would be reviewed: the Information Access Division, the Software and Systems Division, and the Statistical Engineering Division. The following ITL divisions were not reviewed because they had recently been reorganized (NIST plans to request their review in the future): the Applied and Computational Mathematics Division, the Computer Security Division, and the Advanced Networking Technologies Division. In order to accomplish the assessment, the NRC assembled a panel of 22 volunteers, whose expertise matches that of the work performed by ITL staff.[3]

On June 9-11, 2015, the panel assembled for two and a half days at the NIST facility, during which it received, in a plenary session, welcoming remarks from the NIST Associate Director for Laboratory Programs, heard an overview presentation by ITL management, and attended an interactive session with ITL management. Each panel member was assigned to one of the three division review teams whose expertise matched that of the work performed in three divisions of ITL: the Information Access Division, the Software and Systems Division, and the Statistical Engineering Division. The division review teams separately attended division-level presentations and visited division laboratories. The panel also met in a closed session to deliberate on its findings and to define the contents of this assessment report.

The panel's approach to the assessment relied on the experience, technical knowledge, and expertise of its members. The panel reviewed selected examples of the technical research performed at ITL; because of time constraints, it was not possible to review ITL programs and projects exhaustively. The examples reviewed by the panel were selected by ITL. The panel's goal was to identify and report salient examples of accomplishments, challenges, and opportunities for improvement with respect to the factors suggested above by the Director of NIST. These examples are intended collectively to portray an overall impression of the laboratory, while preserving useful suggestions specific to the projects and programs that the panel examined. The panel applied a largely qualitative rather than quantitative approach to the assessment.

Given the necessarily broad and nonexhaustive nature of the review, omission in this report of any particular ITL program or project should not be interpreted as implying any negative reflection on the omitted program or project.

---

[3] See on the NIST Information Technology Laboratory homepage for information on organization and programs at http://www.nist.gov/itl/, accessed July 3, 2015.

2

Information Access Division

INTRODUCTION

The activities of the Information Access Division (IAD), which has about 90 personnel, are organized along four themes: multimedia information, information retrieval, image processing, and visualization and usability. The research teams enjoy broad peer recognition while supporting the NIST's vision of information technology (IT) in measurement science overall and in measurement science for information technology. The core competencies and facilities in this division are strong, and interactions with other parts of NIST and the ITL are evident, if not always formalized. The following sections in this chapter critique the work in the IAD along the requested dimensions of technical programs, scientific expertise, facilities and resources, and dissemination of outputs. Examples of the division's work are discussed as are ways that the division could enhance the effectiveness, relevance, and recognition of its program while continuing its fine record of success.

ASSESSMENT OF TECHNICAL PROGRAMS

Accomplishments

Community Leadership

IAD personnel provide leadership in the field through a collaborative process that helps define and quantify problems, so that communities of interest can address them. Some of the efforts lead to proposed standards and to standards accepted by outside standards development organizations (SDOs), such as the International Organization for Standardization (ISO) and the Institute of Electrical and Electronics Engineers (IEEE). In some cases, as in the exchange of forensic transactions, ITL laboratory is itself the SDO. This is a valuable service that the IAD carries out in an excellent manner.

There are examples in this collaborative program where ITL and the IAD visibly drive the creation or advancement of important fields. One such example is the Text Retrieval Conference (TREC). Over the past 25 years, the IAD has used the TREC platform to advance the metrics of performance in text retrieval. In particular, the community has moved from simple measures of precision estimates based on simple pooling of test run data to bootstrapping of test runs that consider interactions among query, system, and documents.

In the case of TREC for Video (TRECVID), the IAD has facilitated the identification of key tasks in video retrieval for defining system performance. Today these include semantic indexing, instance search, surveillance event detection, multimedia event detection, and event recounting. These are all tasks that the video retrieval community has accepted as a valid testing methodology for video retrieval systems.

In collaborating with the community, the IAD has repeatedly demonstrated its ability to bring about shared and sustainable leadership, affected by collaboration with the relevant community. Examples are the TREC steering committee, Interoperable Iris Exchange (IREX) iris studies, and ISO SC37 standards for biometrics. These collaborations cover the range of problem definition, creation of data sets with ground truths, and performance metrics. The IAD has helped carry the problem areas to the point where the community can take over the effort, when NIST involvement needs to decrease or end. In this connection, the IAD tends to maintain an effective balance between ongoing areas and new areas that emerge or are mandated.

Competitions, Metrics, and Usability

The IAD has facilitated competitions with results that demonstrate state of the art in the field. Many competitions have high barriers to entry such as cost of equipment or hours of tests required. The IAD has successfully lowered the barriers to entry in some instances.

In the speaker recognition evaluation, the IAD has contributed by providing compact i-vectors rather than terabytes of raw speech data, which would have required substantial computational processing as well as storage to reach the point where analysis could be performed. IAD built the Speaker Recognition I-Vector challenge. In machine translation (MT), the IAD instigated the creation of open-source MT toolkits to lower barriers for entry. The IAD also created "light" track alternatives to large government evaluations (such as at the Defense Advanced Research Projects Agency [DARPA]) so that small laboratories and researchers can participate at some level and contribute diverse and valuable ideas. For example, since 2006, the IAD has run open-MT evaluations parallel to the Global Autonomous Language Exploitation (GALE) and Broad Operational Language Translation (BOLT) evaluations by DARPA.

The IAD has driven the development of a very broad range of new metrics, practices, and tools in information science and technology. Examples are numerous: methods for assessing the strengths of passwords, ways to estimate recall, methods of handling large data sets, human-targeted translation error rate, identification of information intrinsic to latent fingerprints, quality covariates for biometrics, and biometric aging. To explain one contribution: the Metrics for Machine Translation Challenge (MetricsMaTr) evaluations evaluated machine translation metrics that led to the development of alternative automated MT metrics. In summary, the IAD has played a unique and sustained role in focusing worldwide efforts on new metrics and in building machine translation metrics through launching and managing metrics competitions. The multimedia technology contributions of the IAD are complemented by leadership in the topic of visualization and usability. As an example, the IAD was instrumental in creating the biometrics usability field through studies such as those that discovered optimal heights and angles for security scanners at port of entry kiosks.

Opportunities and Challenges

Data-Driven Information Science

A data-driven approach is critical to advancing the field of information science and technology. The IAD team is starting to make an important contribution in this regard. The team is actively engaged in generating appropriate data sets and ground truths, running meaningful tests, and facilitating new web-based data sites. This direction is very positive. There is also an opportunity for the IAD to expand its vision beyond labeled data to include live data and to establish a methodology where larger numbers of candidate algorithms can be investigated through continuous evaluations. This is an industry-wide opportunity and trend, with implications for how to address ground truths and atypical events.

Baseline Implementations

A useful service that the IAD provides is harvesting and providing baseline implementation information to spur further research—supporting the concept of "building on the shoulders of others." The challenge is how to extend this from a closed environment to a larger community of researchers, thus lowering the bar for introducing novel ideas into the mix. On a related theme, many researchers now offer open-source or matrix laboratory (MATLAB®) implementations that allow for quick and easy testing. However, the licensing arrangements can be foggy, and there is a wide variance with respect to the quality of implementation and documentation. The IAD could take a role in helping to harvest these implementations with an eye toward persistence and reliability, and in leveraging open-source environments such as Python that offer useful ways to bundle together data, access methods, and explanatory text.

Tools for Security Policy

IAD's work on the creation of tools for security policy and the representation of these tools in a form that permits agencies to simplify their password definition rules represents a very promising opportunity. Currently, the rules are ambiguous and too complex for system users to comprehend, and this seems to be an obstacle to the application of appropriate security practices government-wide. The IAD tool to clarify password rules promises to reduce this kind of obstacle. A further development of this tool, with appropriate explanatory text, could become an industry resource for citizen-facing government and institutional services, and for consumer-facing commercial firms.

Common Industry Format-Plus

The Common Industry Format (CIF) [ISO/IEC 25062:2006 Software Engineering–Software Product Quality Requirements and Evaluation (SQuaRE)] for usability test reports has been successful. The CIF for summative usability test reports is now in use across industry for safety-related usability certification of electronic health record systems, for usability and accessibility testing and certification of voting systems, and for usability testing of biometric systems. However, there is the question of whether that tool needs to be updated. The CIF focuses on speed, accuracy, and satisfaction with how systems support human work. In the past decade, other important aspects of user experience have gained commercial importance, such as completeness (rather than only speed) of learning, comprehension, and engagement (rather than only accuracy) in game-playing. As design becomes more important in commercial and recreational applications and educational settings for both formal schooling and lifelong learning, factors such as psychophysiological indicators of cognitive load, enjoyment, and other hedonic qualities are becoming increasingly relevant. There is rich measurement literature for these topics, but the unique capabilities of the IAD and ITL are needed to transform research into a more complete metrology of user experience, as measured through the holistic testing of usability and user engagement.

Health Informatics

The health informatics arena represents both an opportunity and a challenge. The Electronic Health Record (EHR) program is not yet quantitatively driven. This was attributed by the IAD to the circumstance that real data arrived late in the process, after a 4-year procurement and Institutional Review Board (IRB) delay. This is a mandated project, and if process indeed hinders its progress, ITL needs to address those problems, in collaboration with NIST leadership, perhaps at the level of the U.S. Congress. If the delay continues, the credibility of NIST could suffer.

Conclusions

The technical programs in the IAD are in general well organized, well staffed, and appropriate to the mission of ITL and IAD.

It is important that IAD maintain its momentum and leadership in its many successful activities but also consider the new opportunities that have been described above. This will be important to ensure success in a rapidly changing science and technology landscape.

It is also important that the division management review programs to identify those that need additional methodology or rigor and those that face challenging adoption paths. Such critical review could lead to the identification of needed resources not found at the division level.

The EHR program, for example, would benefit from a critical review. The addition of new emphases to the Text Retrieval Conference (TREC) Clinical Decision Support tracks would add value to the division's EHR work. Developing health data sets that can be used by the health informatics community would link the 25-year impact of TREC to increasingly important challenges in electronic health records.

PORTFOLIO OF SCIENTIFIC EXPERTISE

Accomplishments

The IAD is a recognized leader in impactful standards activities and conferences. Evidence of recognition appears in many forms, such as program committee selection, conference leadership, and awards. As one example, TREC methods and results have been applauded by the search industry (Google's chief economist), been credited with a 5:1 economic return in an RTI International study,[1] and cited in a federal case.[2]

The IAD personnel have deep expertise in creating metrics and best practices for many classes of information applications. They have the core competency for continuing their mission in the next generation of multimedia and multimodal technologies. It is impressive that the IAD has been able to attract and retain personnel who are among the best in the world in their fields. The fairly recent creation of new programs in open data, big data, data science, privacy, and video is noteworthy and indicative of a broad intellectual base in the IAD.

Opportunities and Challenges

There is an opportunity to enhance core capabilities in several areas where the IAD aspires to make a major contribution. The Data Science program affords an opportunity to develop expertise in big data, linked data, unintended relations, and data mining. In the Privacy program, there is the continuing challenge of deidentification and usable interface controls for privacy settings. In Public Safety, where there is a great societal need and infusion of significant funding in the pipeline, current IAD staff will need to be augmented in terms of scope as well as agility in new scientific areas.

The IAD and the Statistical Engineering Division (SED) have recent, ongoing, and planned collaborations in the following data science projects: identifying face quality and factor measures for video using the point-and-shoot challenge (PaSC) video data, fingerprint database mining for performance assessment of non-parametric likelihood ratios for expressing weight of evidence, statistical analysis methods for evaluating automated text translation systems, measuring the usability and security

---

[1] B.R. Rowe, D.W. Wood, A.N. Link, and D.A. Simoni, Economic Impact Assessment of NIST's Text REtrieval Conference (TREC) Program: Final Report, RTI Project Number 0211875, RTI International, Research Triangle Park, N.C., December 2010, http://www.rti.org/publications/abstract.cfm?pubid=16086.

[2] Stanley v. Pipe, D. Md. (2008). Memorandum and order.

of permuted passwords on mobile platforms, and advanced statistical metrology for information retrieval. Taking advantage of all opportunities for collaboration between these divisions would be beneficial to both.

Addressing outcome measures beyond the CIF, discussed above, is a fundamental scientific opportunity. It is also a necessary evolution of the technical program if the IAD wants to be a player in topics such as educational effectiveness, game-playing experience, social engagement in media, social networking statistics, and citizen engagement in government services. These represent a reasonable extrapolation of IAD activity, but the core expertise will need to be enhanced with respect to expertise and number of researchers.

Conclusions and Recommendations

The portfolio of scientific expertise is appropriate and impressive for the traditional areas that the IAD focuses on, but core capabilities need to be enhanced in areas where the IAD aspires to make an important contribution.

Recommendation: The Information Access Division should review the current and proposed portfolios and examine the adequacy of its core competencies for ambitious new programs like data science, health informatics, and public safety.

Supporting the standards process places resource and attention-span demands on personnel. One option to reduce the demands could be to turn over standards materials to ISO and other SDOs. However, this approach is sometimes associated with update cycles that are too long and possibly too onerous to meet the original intent of the standard, and it entails risk to IAD credibility.

Recommendation: The Information Access Division (IAD) should continually consider the pros and cons of turning over standards materials—for example, the Common Industry Format (CIF)—to the International Organization for Standardization (ISO) and other standards development organizations (SDOs). If the ISO-SDO channel remains the best or only approach, the IAD should consider how to plan proactively for updates as appropriate and should propose updates to the controlling SDO(s) whenever IAD efforts indicate that they are needed or desired by the user community.

ADEQUACY OF FACILITIES, EQUIPMENT, AND HUMAN RESOURCES

Accomplishments

There are notable examples of good infrastructure available for the IAD, such as the Biometric Research Laboratory. Also impressive is a well-cultivated mechanism to expanded reach and impact through off-campus centers of excellence such as the effort with the University of Maryland and the use of cross-organizational virtual teams within ITL and across NIST.

Opportunities and Challenges

The IAD team plays a significant role as leaders and shepherds of their communities of expertise. To fulfill this role with timeliness and excellence, seamless interaction and agility are critical success factors. As such, operational latencies in IRB or travel approval processes can be first-order detriments.

Maximization of impact depends on continued cross-division collaboration and resource allocations. In a strategy that was described by IAD during the review, there appeared to be a major focus in the first one or two years of a new business area, followed by a reliance on the momentum and eventual allocation of resources to the budget. This might be a process worthy of more attention. Ideally, practices would be formalized in a way that permits their reuse for subsequent cross-division projects.

Conclusions and Recommendations

The facilities, equipment, and human resources are strong assets of the IAD. As areas such as health informatics gain importance, there seems to be a tendency to make do with the core talent areas rather than hiring specialists (trained biomedical informaticians and health data scientists) permanently or even for shorter times. This practice needs to be reconsidered in the strategic planning of the division. A prime example of this need is the EHR team.

Recommendation: The Information Access Division (IAD) should bolster the electronic health record team to ensure that this high-profile work is well supported in terms of information technology rigor as well as domain expertise. IAD should add scientists or contractors with strong clinical experience, include all stakeholders (physicians, nurses, technicians, pharmacists, and patients) in its empirical investigations, and participate in medical informatics communities such the American Medical Informatics Association (AMIA) and the congressionally chartered Patient-Centered Outcomes Research Institute (PCORI). Internally, the IAD should collaborate closely with the Text Retrieval Conference (TREC) team on medical tracks.

Collaborative teamwork with scientists and engineers inside and outside of IAD, including virtual teamwork and in-person interactions, is of fundamental importance to the work of the IAD staff.

Recommendation: To maximize the mechanism of virtual teams and to foster contacts with other laboratories, IAD should give greater consideration to the formulation of clear policies and processes that support sabbaticals and appropriate travel.

It would be helpful to create an IT sandbox, using computational resources not connected to the core NIST infrastructure, to leverage infrastructure in creative and flexible ways that a general information security policy might inhibit.

DISSEMINATION OF OUTPUTS

Accomplishments

The IAD has played key roles in creating standards for almost 30 years. Examples cover a broad range, from usability test reporting to biometric information exchange. The CIF for software usability testing and reporting, which started in what is now the IAD, has become an ISO standard (SC7 (CIF) ISO/IEC 25062:2005). The standard for the exchange of fingerprint data, which also started in the IAD (when NIST was the National Bureau of Standards) as a Federal Bureau of Investigation (FBI)-funded project, has remained an American National Standards Institute (ANSI) standard since it was first approved in 1986. This standard has been updated several times to the current version (ANSI/NIST-ITL 1-2011 Update 2013). It has been used internationally, in at least 50 countries and by Interpol, for the exchange of biometric and forensic data in and among criminal justice systems, applicant screening systems, and border-crossing applications. IAD has also worked with the Election Assistance

Commission to develop usability and accessibility standards for voting systems (Chapter 3 of the Voluntary Voting System Standards) as part of the NIST Voting Program.

In further support of standards, the IAD has developed and made available software trackers of standard conformance that are also widely used.

The IAD has also developed broadly usable IT tools for parsing and displaying password policies.

Opportunities and Challenges

Web-based tools can be used to broaden participation in workshops and short conferences and to disseminate the results and proceedings. This has been done recently for the NIST conference "Improving Biometric and Forensic Technology: The Future of Research Datasets."

The culture of IAD seems to emphasize highlighting the successes of others. This is very conducive to building a community spirit, but it needs to coexist with better marketing of the fundamental value that IAD personnel contribute.

Conclusions and Recommendations

The IAD value proposition with standards and conformance tool sets is outstanding and deserves continued nurturing and support. Its dissemination process would be enhanced by greater use of Internet-based methods.

Recommendation: The Information Access Division should apply more Internet-based methods to its dissemination and outreach process. Such methods as webinars, virtual meetings, and recordings should be considered.

The IAD has a fine record of recognition and engagement. There is an opportunity to gain even broader recognition for the value of the IAD and to engage the even larger community that could benefit from IAD contributions. This will need an effort on the part of the IAD leadership to engage in assertive marketing, including continuously updated website presentations of citations and praise. Some existing examples of such citations come from diverse constituencies such as the private sector and federal court case literature.

3

Statistical Engineering Division

INTRODUCTION

As observed in a National Research Council report,[1] the Statistical Engineering Division (SED) has nearly a 70-year history of

> Consistent and fundamental contributions to the central mission of NIST through the development and application of statistical methodology for metrology. This methodology supports the basic NIST activities of producing measurements and quantifying their associated uncertainties... The SED advances its mission of supporting research in measurement science, technology, and the production of standard reference materials (SRMs), through numerous scientific collaborations within NIST and externally. The SED conducts statistical research and provides important training and educational activities within and beyond NIST. It serves as a unique national and international resource for the metrology and standards communities and more broadly in high profile contexts where an acknowledged impartial broker of data analysis and interpretation is needed.

ASSESSMENT OF TECHNICAL PROGRAMS

Accomplishments

The SED is well-aligned and effective in its support of the main NIST missions. It currently conducts a wide variety of technical efforts, including classical statistical metrology projects such as mass calibration weighing designs, testing standards for cardiac leads, and laboratory experimentation for nanotoxicology. Other work supports national and international best statistical practices in metrology and the development of new methods of measurement and uncertainty quantification for important specialized technical applications. Current examples cover a broad range of scientific projects, including greenhouse gas emissions, U.S. extreme wind speeds, shape metrology, and quantitative imaging of materials, as well as several projects related to the current NIST priority in forensic science, including analysis for low-template deoxyribonucleic acid (DNA) traces, firearms and tool marks, and general modeling and inference for problems in forensic science.

The SED technical efforts are technically challenging and are well executed. Methodology that is developed for and applied to these challenges is sound and of high quality, equivalent to that of the best U.S. national laboratories and best industrial research facilities. In light of the unique mission of NIST and the role played by the SED in NIST, the division is a one-of-a-kind national resource.

---

[1] National Research Council, *Assessment of the National Institute of Standards and Technology Information Technology Laboratory—Fiscal Year 2011*, The National Academies Press, Washington, D.C., p. 30.

Opportunities and Challenges

The SED continues to have a low profile in the national and international technical statistics community. Some existing projects with concrete internal or subject-matter deliverables could be developed further or studied methodologically on a deeper level, which could lead to their publication in the mainstream statistical literature and thereby give the SED greater visibility.

Conclusions and Recommendations

SED could more fully benefit from and contribute to current statistical research.

Recommendation: The Statistical Engineering Division should take steps to raise its profile through technical publications in statistics venues and through educational efforts to improve the awareness of statistics educators of the vital role of measurement in data collection and the role of statistics in good measurement.

PORTFOLIO OF SCIENTIFIC EXPERTISE

Accomplishments

The division's scientific expertise in statistics for metrology continues to be among the best in the world. The division strongly supports the larger NIST organization's programs.

Opportunities and Challenges

It appears that the demands and pressures of important NIST project work presently militate against SED's full engagement with the statistical research community.

Conclusions and Recommendations

Attention to both metrology and the basic statistics field needs to be a division priority in order to move both areas forward and guarantee ongoing excellence in supporting NIST priorities.

Recommendation: The Statistical Engineering Division should seek stronger ties with the statistical research community in terms of both publications and human resources.

ADEQUACY OF FACILITIES, EQUIPMENT, AND HUMAN RESOURCES

Accomplishments

Previous reviews have consistently recommended increases in technical staffing for the SED. Good progress has been made since the last review in 2011: The number of technical staff has increased from 23 to 25.[2]

---

[2] National Research Council, *An Assessment of the National Institute of Standards and Technology Information Technology Laboratory: Fiscal Year 2011*, The National Academies Press, Washington, D.C., 2011.

Opportunities and Challenges

The number of staff continues to be a primary concern for the SED. Sixty-five percent of the technical staff (16 of 25) will become eligible for retirement in the next 5 years. Technical staffing on important projects and in vital areas is very thin (often only one person per project), making the organization quite brittle. Continued hiring is essential into the foreseeable future, at least at the pace of the last 4 years, during which four permanent employees and one guest were hired.

Conclusions and Recommendations

Progress has been made on human resource issues since the 2011 review, but important challenges remain.

Recommendation: In hiring permanent employees, the Statistical Engineering Division (SED) should focus attention on (1) ensuring corporate memory of and expertise in the fundamental ongoing National Institute of Standards and Technology standard reference material (SRM), calibration, and the experimental design work that has always been part of the SED portfolio, and on developing new capabilities in priority areas such as shape metrology and greenhouse gas monitoring, which seem to be particularly thinly staffed; (2) maintaining high overall technical competence; (3) improving staff diversity; and (4) balancing emphases on the noncore and core areas—for example, while forensics is a current laboratory-wide priority and SED is a key participant, when hiring for forensics the SED should address general expertise, so that other more thinly staffed critical areas are not neglected.

Recommendation: The Statistical Engineering Division should invigorate its program of graduate student internships to include two to four Ph.D. students per summer, and it should begin to develop a much broader and stronger program of visiting faculty researchers.

DISSEMINATION OF OUTPUTS

Accomplishments

The SED research programs are clearly driven by stakeholder needs. The division has responded effectively to government priorities such as those related to greenhouse gas emissions and forensic science. Its publications are effective in the metrological literature and for stakeholders.

Opportunities and Challenges

Strong contributions to the statistical literature improve and maintain engagement with the statistical research community and will, over time, improve the methods being brought into SED work. Such efforts come at the expense of time on other projects and therefore require division- and ITL-level support.

Conclusions and Recommendation

Publications, presentations, interaction with visiting researchers, and sponsoring internships are important means for engaging with the statistical and metrology communities.

Recommendation: The Statistical Engineering Division should monitor its yearly division total publications in the three categories—subject-matter journals, metrology journals, and statistics journals—and external research presentations, research visitor days, and internships sponsored.

4

Software and Systems Division

INTRODUCTION

The Software and Systems Division (SSD) has to respond with an adaptive, nimble strategy to congressional mandates imposed on NIST. The division needs to evaluate each mandate within the context of its mission and expertise, leveraging staff and expertise to continue pursuing a mix of tactical and strategic initiatives. This includes recruitment and cultivation of staff with the requisite skills for those initiatives.

The SSD is engaged in several high profile areas, notably in voting, health IT, and cyberphysical systems (CPS). Failure, even in part, in any one of these areas would have profound implications for the SSD, ITL, and NIST. In each case, it is crucial that the SSD, in collaboration with ITL and NIST management, delineate the risks and rewards within the context of an organizational strategy. By defining the stakeholders and success metrics (e.g., customer satisfaction, standard development, uptake and adoption), it can match competence and resources to the risks and rewards.

In line with the charge to the panel provided by the NIST Director, the assessment of the SSD focused on the following criteria:

- *The unique NIST mission and its relationship to the broader articulation of the NIST/ITL strategy (i.e., non-duplicative of other academic, laboratory, or industrial efforts).* Of these, standards development is the most impactful—followed by the advancement of practice for measurement, evaluation, and interoperation support—because small NIST groups can have extraordinary influence by leveraging a unique body of competence, institutional knowledge, and outreach capability.
- *The technical excellence of the project and its team.* Concomitantly, projects need to draw on the core intellectual expertise and mission focus of the SSD, with skills aligned with the mission, objectives, and mandates.
- *The degree of community involvement,* balancing leadership and impartial convening for standards development and community engagement.

ASSESSMENT OF TECHNICAL PROGRAMS AND PORTFOLIO OF SCIENTIFIC EXPERTISE

The projects presented by the SSD staff span a wide range, from individual staff projects that are preliminary research investigations to broader initiatives that are coupled to external communities.

Medical Imaging

Accomplishments

The computational science metrology effort focuses primarily on computational science and measurement issues related to analysis of biomedical microscopy data. Analysis of multiscale imaging data is an increasingly important component in many areas, including biomedicine and materials science. In this class of challenging applications, a very large number (10^9 or more) of objects need to be segmented and tracked over time. Characterizing the agreement between segmentation and tracking algorithms is a crucial and challenging component of this effort, as is the need to quickly integrate and stitch disjoint patches of image data. The computational metrology SSD group has done admirable work in attracting strong scientific collaborators in the stem cell therapy area and in collaborating with this group to generate both publicly distributed software and published scientific results.

Opportunities and Challenges

The quality of this work is extraordinarily high, but the group would likely increase the impact by broadening focus to supporting a broader range of scientific driving problems. A broader set of microscopy-based applications could be entertained. In addition, the group might consider metrology issues associated with the analysis of other types of imaging. The inherent strengths of the SSD might be best served by a sharper focus on metrology methodology issues and metrology-related imaging standards. A common set of issues arise in the analysis of multiscale imaging data in many diverse application areas; the SSD could potentially play an important role by helping scientific groups realize that they face a common set of metrology and algorithmic challenges.

Voting Security and Verification

In the wake of the vote-counting challenges faced in the 2000 Presidential election, the United States started to pay more attention to its voting processes and technologies. Achieving standards-based practices is challenging, because elections in the United States are carried out by more than 10,000 entities, with wide variations in technical capability and in the number of registered voters per entity.[1] Few of these entities have the budget or skilled personnel to enable them to evaluate new technologies independently or to compare and contrast processes on their own.

Accomplishments

In response to multiple mandates, ITL has assumed an increasingly important role in voting systems since 2002. Voting security and verification is one of the SSD's long-term, priority projects. In response to legislative mandates, it has been sustained over many years, with a strong and steady track record despite considerable oscillations in available funding. SSD reported that standards developed by the program are being widely adopted. Engagement with the large and diverse communities of stakeholders is extensive. The SSD team is responsive to the voting-technology community.

---

[1] According to NIST data, some Northeastern townships have as little as a few hundred voters, while Los Angeles County has about 4.8 million voters supported in 10 languages.

Opportunities and Challenges

Despite the depth and importance of ITL work on voting systems development and implementation, the public profile of the SSD in this area is not high. Among academic institutions, the California Institute of Technology (Caltech), the Massachusetts Institute of Technology (MIT), and Stanford University are better known for their work on voting. The SSD could do more in the development of effective and publicly disseminated software test tools and methodologies.

Challenges remain regarding the mechanisms through which confident assurance judgments can be made for particular voting devices. These include how device vendors can effectively support the process. This needs to extend beyond mainstream vulnerability scans and penetration testing. These tests address primarily vulnerabilities already identified by the cybersecurity community and for which there is experience in established mainstream computing systems. In general, however, they do not provide positive assurances regarding either other exploitable flaws or reliability challenges unrelated to cybersecurity. Voting systems are a mission-critical feature of the U.S. democratic process, and the thresholds for acceptance need to be high, even if this means compromising on added technical features. In particular, acceptance evaluation needs to be accomplished through techniques more invasive than the block-box evaluations typically used to test system-level penetration in business and consumer systems.

ITL is in the important position of facilitating the dialog between the vendor community, which seeks to protect its intellectual property, and voting officials, who seek to make confident judgments regarding the fitness of candidate voting devices. This process of balancing interests requires a high level of expertise as well as an engaged neutral stance and an ability to engage effectively with diverse stakeholders. The SSD voting team has these characteristics, and, consequently, it has a nationally significant role.

There is nonetheless a fragility to the SSD voting team, which consists of a small group of capable and dedicated individuals. Although the team is augmented by staff from the Information Access Division, the Statistical Engineering Division, and the Computer Security Division, it was not apparent during the review which mechanism is used to recruit and develop the necessary bench strength.

Cloud Standards

Accomplishments

SSD's work on cloud computing standards has had a substantial impact on government and industry, both within the United States and internationally. Indeed, SSD's body of definitions related to the various kinds of cloud computing—its reference architecture—is now internationally accepted, and it has led to a voluntary, consensus ISO standard. As an impartial and regular convener of cloud service providers and consumers, the SSD continues to provide a forum for technical interchange and a venue for development of an evolving series of standards and a reference architecture. Reflecting interest levels and SSD credibility, the working groups on architectures and services, metrics, security, and interoperability continue to attract hundreds of participants.

This work on cloud computing is driven by the relatively high level of commitment and risk associated with cloud adoption decisions, both in industry and in government. Decisions associated with the adoption of cloud computing encompass choices regarding the structure and location of organizational data and the selection of computing paradigms. The principal decisions are architectural, but there are also decisions related to sourcing, with options ranging from vendor clouds (such as from Amazon, Google, and Microsoft) to shared or dedicated organizational clouds. Many criteria influence decisions, and the engineering trade-offs are complex and are conducted in a technological environment of both evolutionary and rapid change.

Cloud computing is significant because it has emerged as the dominant pathway to scale in computing resources. Cloud architectures offer not just the ability to manifest scale but also, separately, the ability to rapidly scale up (or down) in the face of changing computational demands. While "the cloud" can also be a potential pathway to enormous cost savings due to the ability to share resources and the balancing of loads, any sharing of resources creates the possibility of security and reliability issues. Moreover, importantly, cloud computing is a pathway to flexibility and adaptability of data-intensive and computationally intensive systems and capabilities. This flexibility is increasingly important for a wide range of corporate and agency mission systems.

Opportunities and Challenges

In the federal government, cloud adoption is perceived as having both high benefit and high risk. Identifying the decision criteria and navigating the trade-offs that realize the benefits with acceptable risk requires a high level of technical understanding. The SSD is facilitating this process by working with industry to assist in the decision and adoption process, identifying the full range of criteria and, importantly, collaborating to develop the necessary metrics and guidance. This is creating a benefit for a broad range of stakeholders.

SSD expertise and activities in this space have helped shape U.S. government cloud adoption. With respect to U.S. federal cloud strategy, the NIST initiative is the only deep effort, and it has the potential to shape the decision space for cloud engagements across multiple federal agencies.

Software Assurance

Accomplishments

Software assurance is one of the most critical challenges for software-reliant systems of all kinds. It is key for cybersecurity defense, safety-critical systems, infrastructural systems, national security systems, and mainstream personal consumer systems. Software assurance failures are unfortunately ubiquitous, even in the most heavily evaluated systems.

The SSD software assurance project has done an excellent job of building useful data sets that can benefit producers of software tools and in raising awareness about the existence of these data sets. This includes databases of common software risks and security vulnerabilities and of test cases.

The SSD software assurance project focuses specifically on tools for static software analysis. There are many other critical aspects of assurance practice, with broad-scope models such as the Microsoft Security Development Lifecycle and the Building Security in Maturity Model evaluation framework. These provide frameworks through which a wide range of specific practices can be integrated into an overall process of development, evaluation, and modernization, with process models ranging from traditional linear and V models to DevOps and small-team-agile models. Choices that influence the potential to achieve reliable assurance judgments include selection of programming languages, tools, and models for requirements, and design to testing approaches, inspection, analysis, and runtime monitoring and logging.

The SSD software assurance activity focuses primarily on static software analysis. This analysis operates at the level of code, usually source code, but there are also analyses directed at object code. Analyses of this kind can address many different categories of defects, and their success can range widely. For each particular quality attribute (i.e., category of defects) covered, diverse success measures are applicable, including rates (and nature) of false positives and false negatives, scalability with respect to performance of the analysis, and composability with respect to software components.

Opportunities and Challenges

The software assurance effort at the SSD builds on the Common Weakness Enumeration and Common Vulnerabilities and Exposures resources from the MITRE Corporation, which are inventories of specific kinds of software weaknesses and instances of vulnerabilities. The SSD effort takes on the challenge of linking these inventories with influences on development and evaluation practice.

Given its scope, the SSD effort is at a high level of quality and responsiveness to its stakeholder community. The effort is known among vendors and many adopters as well. The scope is appropriate and important, since the evaluation frameworks, arguably, are prompting more efficient competition and more rapid innovation. There are questions, however, from the portfolio perspective.

For example, many of the other projects in ITL include the development of tests for conformance to the various standard representations and protocols to support interoperation. Most of these tests are black box—that is, predicated on the tested components being opaque to the test managers. However, this technique is only effective when certain engineering constraints are respected in the development of the black box component; without this, the results may not be sufficiently predictive. These constraints relate to determinism at all levels of design and implementation and to use of physical devices.

More could be done by the SSD in the development of effective and publicly disseminated software test tools and methodologies—for example, for conformance and interoperability testing. The SSD could take a leading role in the development of software test tools.

Software Forensics

Accomplishments

The SSD has several projects related to computer forensics. This is an increasingly important feature of processes associated with criminal investigations and legal discovery as well as the preservation and archiving of electronic documents, data, and other computational assets. Complicating the process is the vast amount of data space dedicated to systems and applications software as well as associated common data assets. Also complicating the process is uncertainty regarding the actions to take, for example, in a law enforcement situation in the immediate moments when computers and mobile devices are seized and potentially volatile data needs to be preserved.

A complete review of the software forensics area could not be conducted, because much of this work is shared with the Cybersecurity Division of ITL, which fell outside the scope of the present review. However, it was noted that the SSD has developed a very large corpus of signatures for applications and standard files. The SSD team is also developing both guidance and test capabilities to facilitate the evaluation of various kinds of forensic tools and capabilities.

Opportunities and Challenges

Matches with items in the corpus of signatures for applications and standard files would enable the forensic process to focus rapidly on data specific to a situation, avoiding the manual process of sifting out common software and data files. The scale of the SSD corpus is growing rapidly. However, there are significant technical challenges to be faced, including the proliferation of versions of frequently released software, the addition of shape shifting and other resiliency features that make fingerprinting more difficult, and the increasing role of cloud and other remote resources in hosting user data.

This latter challenge could drive the need for a significant paradigm shift from the current approach based on signature matching. This is analogous to the challenge faced in the fingerprinting of malware specimens, many of which no longer have a readily identifiable static form.

Cyberphysical Systems and the Internet of Things

The activities in the Internet of Things (IoT) and Cyberphysical Systems (CPS) are a welcome addition to the SSD portfolio, because these domains are important from a technological and industrial point of view. These domains are going to be critical to the future of services and products. The approach taken by the SSD is technically sound and addresses some of the important issues in the area. The industrial relevance of the IoT in the United States is high, as demonstrated by the enormous industrial interest that has resulted in a cacophony of semistandards proposed by many industrial consortia. The consortia were formed to define communication standards, but there is still no clear winner. In this environment, NIST can function as a neutral player to mediate among different camps.

Opportunities and Challenges

On the technical side, the SSD has demonstrated leadership in establishing the smart city grand challenge as well as the CPS Public Working Group (CPS PWG), providing a forum for discussing the CPS reference architecture, security, interoperability, and testing. In this activity, the SSD has gained recognition and engagement in the scientific community. It remains to be seen whether the division can reach the same level of visibility and engagement in the industrial community. It would be beneficial for SSD to engage the community in leveraging the test infrastructure that they are developing. In this respect, the technical capability of the precision timing researchers is high; they showed excellent knowledge of the field and overall competence spanning many areas.

Electronic Health Records

Multiple major drivers for change face the nation as it seeks to create a sustainable learning health and healthcare delivery system. The nation is moving to an accountable care organization structural model for the health and care of defined populations, with payment based on documented value relating to outcomes, services, and relevant quality and safety. To achieve the desired outcomes, patients and communities need to become active partners, working with relevant interprofessional teams relating to health and care. The nation is also moving toward care based on precision medicine, where care is increasingly based on individual characteristics at the molecular as well as the societal level (e.g., genomics and epigenetics). With the recent federal major investment in electronic health records(EHRs) and data exchanges, there is an expectation that the big data health information infrastructure necessary for an information and communications ecosystem needed to achieve major progress will be created.

With respect to the big data ecosystem, EHRs and related public health data generators need to be able to create health records from a common data strategy through the nation's recent investments in health information and communication technology (HICT) and biomedical and health informatics (BHI). Critical elements of a learning health and healthcare system include scalable data needed for the following:

- *Care delivery for individuals and populations*, such as Clinical Document Architecture HL7 as well as standards for mobile health monitoring technology, so that the devices are secure and stable in their performance but also capable of interoperability, to enable scaling the data that can also result;
- *Payment,* particularly considering safety, effectiveness, efficiency, timeliness, patient-centeredness, and equitability;
- *Research needs*, particularly for system analytics and process reengineering to move toward clinical precise performance; and

- *Clinical performance of the workforce*, including maintenance of certification and quality performance of individuals and institutions.

Accomplishments

NIST has been performing a mandated role as part of the American Recovery and Reinvestment Act (ARRA) Health Information Technology for Economic and Clinical Health (HITECH) legislation. Specifically, the role relates to supporting the ONC with EHRs and meaningful use. The current staff at the SSD is comprised of capable computer scientists and information technologists, but includes no biomedical/health informaticians.

Opportunities and Challenges

It is not clear that the ONC has a comprehensive strategy that allocates the tasks needed for the nation to achieve interoperable EHRs and EHR systems. Therefore, the SSD is faced with making a strategic choice. One choice is to limit its EHR-related work so that it focuses, essentially, only on relevant but narrow technology issues and does not represent itself as working on meaningful use or interoperability components, which intrinsically involve clinical information relating to decision making and clinical care. Alternatively, the SSD could work through a well-defined and circumscribed agenda coordinated with the other relevant key government agencies, including ONC, the National Library of Medicine (NLM), the National Institutes of Health (NIH), the Agency for Healthcare Research and Quality (AHRQ), and the Food and Drug Administration (FDA). Also, the SSD could consider approaching NLM for collaboration and assistance.

Recommendation: The Software and Systems Division not only should participate in the International Organization for Standardization (ISO)/International Electrotechnical Commission (IEC) joint technical committee working group on the Internet of Things (ISO/IEC JTC 1/WG10) and the Institute of Electrical and Electronics Engineers (IEEE) project on the Standard for an Architectural Framework for the Internet of Things (P2413), but also should reach out to the industrial consortia such as the Industrial Internet Consortium and the Open Interconnect Consortium.

Recommendation: The Software and Systems Division should make open to the scientific and industrial communities the framework that the SSD put together for the Smart Grid, as well as tools and techniques developed in university projects such as PRET (Precision Timed) machines project at the University of California, Berkeley.

Recommendation: The Software and Systems Division should look into growing its approach to timing in connection with Internet of Things applications by considering protocols that are robust to clock drift.

Recommendation: For the electronic health record (HER) the Software and Systems Division (SSD) should define a clear direction that allows it to either focus on limited objectives or add staff of the appropriate types to meet larger expectations. Because focusing on meaningful use of EHRs is intrinsically clinical in nature, the SSD should consider adding clinical informaticians to its staff.

ADEQUACY OF FACILITIES, EQUIPMENT, AND HUMAN RESOURCES

Accomplishments

The SSD project suite spans a wide range that includes improving voting in national and local elections; electronic medical records; and the use of standards in forensics, cybersecurity, and software assurance. Overall, the technical work seems excellent and is conducted by capable staff. There have been substantial accomplishments, especially given the limited available resources and legislative mandates. In addition, based on the projects presented for review, there seems to be an appropriate balance of long-term, short-term, and opportunistic projects. The SSD uses a mix of formal and informal management processes to maintain that balance.

Projects where the SSD engages in standards activities have the most impact, followed by activities focusing on advancing measurement and evaluation capability. These activities leverage a body of expertise and institutional experience at the SSD, magnifying its leverage. Given the limited resources of the SSD, this is particularly important.

Opportunities and Challenges

Key SSD personnel seem to have opportunities to pursue new projects within the limited resources available to them. Continued pressure to take on additional projects could necessitate more formal prioritization criteria and processes and could also hinder the ongoing professional development of technical staff, which is essential, given the pace of technological advances.

Because many staff members are committed to multiple projects and most existing projects are expected to continue for extended periods, the SSD is at or near its capacity to undertake new projects. This fragility of human resources creates project and organizational risk. With limited bench strength, the loss of even one or two individuals could endanger or derail several extant projects.

The SSD seems to attract requests from other parts of NIST that are less capable in computer science. The SSD needs to determine whether this is something NIST management wants to encourage, and whether the SSD mission needs to be made more explicit, so that staffing allocations match the mission. Alternatively, these engagements could be limited to maximize human resource flexibility for core projects. The non-personnel resources (e.g., computing infrastructure and laboratory space) seem adequate but limited. There is little room for contraction of work without adversely affecting current programs, and such contraction could limit uptake of new projects, as do personnel constraints. Conversely, there are important opportunities for the SSD to leverage technical expertise elsewhere in ITL, particularly in the area of cybersecurity. With many SSD activities establishing patterns for future technical development, it is important that they be fully informed regarding considerations of security, as well as functionality, performance, and other quality attributes. This applies, for example, to work related to voting, health data management, and CPS.

The SSD lacks the resources or internal expertise to devote additional effort to outreach and dissemination. Consequently, its work is well regarded within the narrow communities with which the SSD directly interacts, but the work is not known in larger contexts. This outreach would be best undertaken with support from higher organizational levels (e.g., ITL or NIST as a whole) if the organization were to adopt explicit outreach goals in a manner similar to other research-oriented organizations (e.g., NSF and NIH). The work on voting, for example, illustrates the importance of this broader outreach, because it touches on technical as well as social issues.

With respect to its work on electronic health records, coordinated with the work of other relevant key government agencies, the SSD could augment its staff appropriately to address the challenges, with assured funding and explicit roles for multiple years. This would also enable better consistency across those involved in establishing standards for data representation and interoperability.

The SSD could consider approaching NLM for collaboration and assistance. It is possible that NLM could provide one or more clinical informaticians who could work on loan to the SSD effort. In addition, the SSD might consider establishing Intergovernmental Personnel Act (IPA) positions to attract academic medical center-based clinical informaticians to the SSD. The absence of in-house clinical expertise is problematic, because the SSD work will almost certainly be conceived as being broader and demand greater expertise than the current skill set of SSD personnel. Adding some clinical informatics personnel would make great sense. The clinical informaticians need not be physicians, because clinical informatics is an interdisciplinary field; a well-trained nurse informatician may be equally effective. The extramural visibility and importance of the HITECH electronic health record initiative is such that it should only fail on sound merits rather than from lack of internal collaboration and coordination across agencies having the relevant expertise.

DISSEMINATION OF OUTPUTS

The SSD is a gem in the crown of the nation's research laboratories, yet today too few Americans know about its activities and accomplishments despite their being able to enjoy the benefits of SSD's work. A more public face for the SSD would serve it well. That public face should focus on SSD's achievements and their meaning. This visibility would be a vehicle for communicating the benefits of SSD's activities and as a mechanism for shaping public opinion about the SSD's priorities and resource needs.

Other federal agencies and laboratories have highly visible communication and social media outreach strategies. For example, NIH has its foundation;[2] NLM has its Friends of the Library,[3] with a publication for doctor's offices called MedLine Plus; and the Centers for Disease Control and Prevention has a foundation.[4] NSF and the Department of Energy have similar outreach and communication programs to highlight the broad impact of their work on society.

Given SSD's resources, this outreach could take place in collaboration with ITL and NIST as a whole. Individual divisions are too small, and the cross-couplings of projects are too great, for outreach engagement at the division level to be effective. Active communication is an element of strategy; it shapes the environment in which projects are pursued and resources are allocated.

---

[2] See the Foundation for the National Institutes of Health website at http://www.fnih.org/, accessed July 3, 2015.

[3] See the Friends of the National Library of Medicine website at http://www.fnlm.org/, accessed July 3, 2015.

[4] See the CDC Foundation website at http://www.cdcfoundation.org/, accessed July 3, 2015.

Acronyms

AHRQ	Agency for Healthcare Research and Quality
AMIA	American Medical Informatics Association
ANSI	American National Standards Institute
ARRA	American Recovery and Reinvestment Act
BHI	biomedical and health informatics
BOLT	Broad Operational Language Translation
BSIMM	Building Security in Maturity Model
Caltech	California Institute of Technology
CDC	Centers for Disease Control and Prevention
CIF	Common Industry Format
CPS	cyberphysical systems
CPS PWG	CPS Public Working Group
CVE	Common Vulnerabilities and Exposures
CWE	Common Weakness Enumeration
DARPA	Defense Advanced Research Projects Agency
DNA	deoxyribonucleic acid
EHR	electronic health record
FBI	Federal Bureau of Investigation
FDA	Food and Drug Administration
GALE	Global Autonomous Language Exploitation
HICT	health information and communication technology
HITECH	Health Information Technology for Economic and Clinical Health
IAD	Information Access Division
ITL	Information Technology Laboratory
IEEE	Institute of Electrical and Electronics Engineers
IoT	Internet of Things
IPA	Intergovernmental Personnel Act
IRB	Institutional Review Board
IREX	Interoperable Iris Exchange
ISO	International Organization for Standardization
MATLAB®	matrix laboratory
MetricsMaTr	Metrics for Machine Translation Challenge

MIT	Massachusetts Institute of Technology
MT	machine translation
NIH	National Institutes of Health
NIST	National Institute of Standards and Technology
NLM	National Library of Medicine
NRC	National Research Council
ONC	Office of the National Coordinator
PCORI	Patient-Centered Outcomes Research Institute
PRET	Precision Timed
SDL	Security Development Lifecycle
SDO	standards development organization
SED	Statistical Engineering Division
SQuaRE	Software Product Quality Requirements and Evaluation
SRM	standard reference material
SSA	software analysis
SSD	Software and Systems Division
TREC	Text Retrieval Conference
TRECVID	TREC for Video